IF I COULD GIVE YOU A LINE

AKRON SERIES IN POETRY

Titles published since 2014.
For a complete listing of titles published in the series,
go to www.uakron.edu/uapress/poetry.

IF I COULD GIVE YOU A LINE

Carrie Oeding

 The University of Akron Press
Akron, Ohio

ISBN: 978-1-62922-241-7 (paper)
ISBN: 978-1-62922-242-4 (ePDF)
ISBN: 978-1-62922-243-1 (ePub)

LIBRARY OF CONGRESS CATALOGING-IN-PUBLICATION DATA
Names: Oeding, Carrie, author.
Title: If I could give you a line / Carrie Oeding.
Description: First edition. | Akron, Ohio : The University of Akron Press, 2023. |
  Series: Akron series in poetry
Identifiers: LCCN 2022052880 (print) | LCCN 2022052881 (ebook) | ISBN 9781629222417
  (paperback) | ISBN 9781629222424 (pdf) | ISBN 9781629222431 (epub)
Subjects: LCGFT: Poetry.
Classification: LCC PS3615.E35 I37 2023 (print) | LCC PS3615.E35 (ebook) |
  DDC 811/.6—dc23/eng/20221108
LC record available at https://lccn.loc.gov/2022052880
LC ebook record available at https://lccn.loc.gov/2022052881

∞ The paper used in this publication meets the minimum requirements of ANSI/NISO z39.48–1992
(Permanence of Paper).

Cover image: *Rendering of Tower*, by Kelly Goff. Cover design by Amy Freels.

If I Could Give You A Line was designed and typeset in Garamond with
Franklin Gothic titles by Amy Freels and printed on sixty-pound natural
and bound by Baker & Taylor Publisher Services of Ashland, Ohio.

Funding provided in part by a grant from the Rhode Island State Council
on the Arts, through an appropriation by the Rhode Island General
Assembly, a grant from the National Endowment for the Arts and private
funders.

RISCA
Rhode Island State Council On The Arts
Art is the Anchor

Affordable
Learning Initiative
THE UNIVERSITY OF AKRON

Produced in conjunction with the University
of Akron Affordable Learning Initiative. More
information is available at
www.uakron.edu/affordablelearning/

for Viola

CONTENTS

WILL YOU LINE UP THE CHILDREN?

For pigtails, balance beams, cracks to break your mother's back.
    Everything, lines.

I wrote loops, not over and over but forward and forward and
my line was a graphite bow, a graphite flight performing an air show, a
    telephone cord to stories and signatures, a sideways gallop.

Put a word in. Even *bird*. Not even a kind of bird.
I would write that bird to be a lace bird a paltry bird a saffron sparkle word
    bird.

That year all the words would fall into my lines.

Even *chair* for you to sit down while my line kept going.
I would learn cursive and go.
I was a dot in Minnesota on I-90. I had learned about the west and the east.

A ray is a dot with a line leaving it that never ends.

This young thing wants to pirouette on the power lines.
This young thing says his thoughts are kite string.

I am putting children in all of my lines—

I have a tightrope to skim above the sea. An assembly line of square cheese.
Language meet lines. Lines meet language. Those Cy Twombly chalk
squiggles. Knots of excuses. Flâneur through garbage. A stomp to the bus.

Children, fall into me. Make breasts, silhouettes. I've been writing lines all
    of this time.

THE MAKING OF THINGS

—after looking at Richard Long's *A Line Made by Walking*

A man walks through a field and makes a line.

It is made of nothing but breath,

legs, the willingness of soft grasses. The failure of pencils.

The success of pencils. The phrases that failed you,

but you still have a body.

It is a field of wheat and blindfolded children.

This line is made of what you couldn't tag and what you've caught.

It's the envy of skirt slits, pregnancy sticks, ruled paper.

Of wedding aisles and tollbooths.

The envy of waiting. Waiting in line. Waiting in line is the only waiting
    there is.

When you are making a line, you are no longer waiting. When you are no
    longer waiting,

you are waving. You made it! And you're going.

No. Dear poems, you always think first in terms of departure.

I am coming to you. I am not going away!

*

It is so easy. A man walks through a field and makes a line. What else could be made with no hands? Song. I'm becoming all hands, reaching so hard. I'm grabbing every instrument I can find to keep them occupied. What sound am I making? It's hard to think through my own orchestra. Would you please hold this note? One of these instruments? What do you hear? Is this your hand? It takes a little letting go, I guess. And now everything seems difficult and loud.

A man walks through a field and makes a line. I am blowing a horn to make a path that still. I am just sitting next to your table at my table. I'm talking too loudly about how good the food is.

*

I cannot make what I envy. I can pick out eye shadow that's a nice color
and swipe it over my lid without skill. I've had a miscarriage, a pregnancy,
and a birth since my last post. I look at Instagram pics so much that I don't
feel bad about myself. I think I actually look like all of it. I am a clavicle
in a blouse, Delevingne's brows, a knock-off Eames chair that no one sits
on. Sometimes after dinner, for guests, Ray Eames would just place a
floral arrangement in the middle of the table to look at instead of dessert.
She used everything in that house. When I toured it, another tourist
explained to his girlfriend how to improve the architecture. His girlfriend,
not listening like a bucket of fresh ice. If I could place an arrangement of
flowers in here, what would I miss? I am trying to give you something, but
I want envy. I want it neat. I want to feel really bad about myself when
I love something I did not make. I don't usually do anything good with
these feelings. But most of the feelings are good. A poet I really like said
most poets today are just dicking around with voice. That doesn't make me
feel bad about myself. But I'm clearly keeping that line around. Someone
screams something at me while I'm walking the baby. It's unintelligible, and
it is kept, too.

*

This line is not a path. Not a row. Not an aisle of what you need and don't need.

Not a border. Not an alley, a lane, a route. Not direction or division.

Not a luge chute or hiking trail. No corn maze or dark hallway to the video art.

Not a driveway or horse stall or balance beam.

What is a voice in a field? What is a line in a voice? This a voice on the stairs.

*

This line is how I got here. This line is where I'm going. This line I jumped.
   It is going

through me. I am going down it. It has passed me, and I am waiting.

Why does this sound so much like my voice? Because it can't be?

A mark, a division, a line. A line. An obvious he. An obvious lie.

You are so meticulous, this line says.

One problem with being meticulous is that all of me is not.

There are no problems with being a line.

It can talk to you, it can ignore you, reach you, make you speak.

It can be dropped. It can't be held, and we all prefer it that way.

But I have hands and a voice. The line is always hard, even soft lines.

I have you. I am not making you.

I know. And I have to stay here if I want to go anywhere.

I like being had, haved. Halved like the field Richard Long walked.

Walking hand and hand, we don't split anything. I don't feel whole, either.

Whole, as in yet to be touched, pieced. Or am I consumed?

Or what has consumed me, referring to me now as the whole thing gone?

*

I've been here so long people ask how I made this line.

I give them line upon line from someone else's novel.

Okay, they say, we can see this is going somewhere.

I have a longing for what I can't do.

They make suggestions: Finish your novel. Go away. Try drawing.

I take a drawing class. I can't draw.

Everyone else can draw.

Something is on my paper. It looks like drawing.

I am instructed not to look. I chose the right class.

I am drawing. I can't draw. The instructor says I am drawing.

I wait for someone to say I'm not drawing. Someone does say

this is not drawing, but they are talking about my drawing.

Something is on my drawing. It is a line.

I made this line without you. I wasn't really thinking about you, but after I drew it, I wanted you to see.

So I made this line without you, you see?

I drew a line that you couldn't have. Here.

I couldn't have it either. I drew a line, and there was a history

of me in it. I was also falling apart.

Or was it that I had a problem, and I drew a line.

Or was it that I drew a line and then had a problem.

I had a problem that I loved. It was a blank page.

It was a line on a page. It was what I could give.

Just draw a picture. But that is not what drawing is.

I can hardly stop it. Make it. The success

of your lines. I don't. I can hardly touch. And this means I am.

*

I forget the line is simple, but then remember the line is simple.
Someone told me to just go, and things would start happening.
I am saying it all. I am telling someone for the first time.
Someone tells me I am moving. They are not talking to me.
Like, I love that you could care less and couldn't. I feel drawn to it all.
I am paying attention and not learning. What mark did the whistle make?
My friend says any mark is a line. I am elated.
I notice all of the melting is snow.
I start over, but there is still a little bit that I can't totally wipe away.
And there's the dirty towel I used to wipe it. I keep the towel and put it in
    the show.

A BUNCH OF DIFFERENT PARTS CAN MAKE UP
EKPHRASIS, INCLUDING A SCOFF WHEN I ROUND THE
MUSEUM CORNER WITH MY BABY IN THE STROLLER.
OR THE INVISIBLE PUSH TO KEEP MOVING THAT
MEANS KEEP LOOKING, LIKE STOP LOOKING. OR THE
THINGS I THINK OF WHEN I LOOK AT ART AND WON'T
EVER EXPLAIN, EVEN.

Looking, just the idea of it, sounds like a continuous moment or action. An ocean. A fan in July. Planets planeting. But looking isn't even episodic, let alone a stream or line. When I look, I am assembling moving boxes. I am never going to pack. I am away. I am reaching for. I am just reaching for my phone. I'm a row of anything I can't line up. I look like the opposite of stone. I am inside something that is running away from me.

The word mothering sounds like I am always looking at whom I am mothering. An expected rain. A wasteful shower. Making sure the cups are full. Filling to spill. The word mothering sounds like Mary's painted, downward smile. Her always look that we can only discuss as subtle differences, never unexpected, in the permanent collections.

I was in the room. I am in the room. Looking at art. My big foot up to the line. My absence. A description. A description of my description. My wonder. My embarrassment when I take photos of the art. The moment when I don't care who's here. Talking until someone is present. Saying come over here, knowing you can't.

My baby looked like a baby. I was scared of her. Not my baby, just like any red screaming baby, when they put her in my arms. When we took her home, we three were very alone. We kept everyone away for weeks and weeks. Her first outing was the art museum. Her head turned to light in the atrium. The museum was empty, but I still sweat. There are art museums without guards, if you live in the wrong towns. Well that's your choice, they said.

We stand round blankly as walls.

In the museum, I'm not the best student. I look and take notes like a staircase. I have as many feelings as an umbrella that can't be opened. Especially in a museum. I think you'll like this if you are not the best student, either, and want to connect. Here is a box. What does *here* mean? If you are not a student, you are probably a good student. This painting is actually more sculpture, I read.

I stayed long enough to learn about hands. See how Margaret Kilgallen's work, they said, looks like a commercial sign, manufactured. But when you come close, you can see the waver, the hand.

We don't like a waver if we don't want it there. We like it when we don't expect it. When it doesn't disappoint, and we didn't think it could have. When we are already looking. Not in love, but something a little better than that. Just looking. When you are in love a waver doesn't seem good. Unless you are more than in love, then it's a wag. If you are talking about love, you are just annoying whomever you are talking to.

Heather wrote that she was most surprised by a new presence. Once there wasn't anyone, and then there was someone. I thought about what this would be like. I waited in that way that's just living, like being pregnant. I was pregnant. Looking at Heather's Facebook posts on what it's like to be a new parent that I just liked and waited to come true.

New statue.

Looking while mothering sounds like you are kidding yourself. Sounds like you are a bad mother. Sounds like you aren't doing anything except seeing food on faces. You are leaving the show with no memory.

Everything now as *rückenfigur*.

Someone is the artist, someone is the art, someone is the writer, someone is the poem, someone is the reader, someone is the listener, someone is taking pictures, someone is guarding, someone is cataloguing. Someone drapes a blanket over all of us. It's Viola. She is making a tent.

Who is here? My neighbor is playing his oboe next door. It doesn't sound like a baby crying, like I read once in a story. Something must exist that just wants to be near it.

Carrying sounds invisible. In the museum we read that for Do Ho Suh's installation, "New York City Apartment, Apartment A, 348 West 22nd Street, New York, NY 10011, USA," he measured the dimensions to his old New York basement apartment and recreated it in silk. Measuring is displacement but sounds like mending.

An artist tells me when he read to his child, every time he turned a page his son was learning about time. I read to Viola for almost two years before I realize I never really get to look at the pictures.

I just want to be near the art. I can't really look, because Viola is two. I'm here to be near something. I don't know if I want to know what that is. I can't stop the stroller for long, or she will scream. She'd rather walk herself. Desire seems like a very clear idea—you want this person, this object, this place. I'm happy to be near something that should be given more time. I don't think anything comes after this.

Watching a baler baling hay is not like looking at art. But it was what I saw. Perfectly packed rectangles in rows, waiting to be picked up. And rows of corn and beans. Years and years of rows. We walked beans, which means we walked down the rows of soybeans looking for weeds to pull. Helping dad's crop yield more crop. This part wants to come into the poem not like a weed.

If I ever get an artwork to speak, I hope it just lets its cold teeth chatter.

We react *yes* or *no* to the art within a few seconds of being in front of it, like we do toward a person. Whatever sprouted in the garden. But I didn't think either when Viola was pulled out of me, and I saw her headed my way.

We list everything we saw today. We talk about our favorites as if we will go back. As if this is about distance and not turning pages.

I KEPT A VOICE IN MY PEACOCK

It said it wasn't a peacock. It was a map.
It said it was meant to be read. I read my peacock
and got lost. Peacocks don't roam. I got lost on very little.
I wanted more, so I left my voice. I didn't have any
plumage, so I shouted blue, blue, blue, and hoped someone would notice
I was doing all of this without a voice. I hoped someone would notice.
It's shameful to want people to notice you're lost, lost and blue, and
    pluming with effort.
When someone finally asked if I was lost, I said no. I have all the love I
    need.
The people who love me don't ask where I'm going.

But unlike my peacock, I am unable to say what I am.
Only the effortless don't need to make promises.

ANY TIME YOU WANT, YOU CAN SEE MOTHERS WIPING

You can be sitting with a friend, talking about how you recently

saw a mother wiping everything, then turn to your left to see

everything was not wiped, as there is a mother next to a garbage can, wiping it
before her child throws something away. One is wiping a child's face
before it is dirty. One wipes everything but memory. The ceiling is dirty. And another mother,

wiping all of the trains that will take you somewhere. There's an arm reaching across the aisle with a wipe. Surely it is a mother's arm, as mothers' arms look like arms that wipe, which look like barges. Two mothers are wiping the journey. One is wiping a drift while another is wiping a compassed direction. And too many to count are on the floor, wiping the marbles that will roll and kiss something not wiped.

One wipes away a season until she is wiping a new season in. What will shine? I don't know, as mothers don't have time to polish.

You will not see them. There's a toy you step over. But you will have seen enough. You know what's important to them, without ever looking, or knowing.

What's also hard to see

is that they never wipe down things they shouldn't. Like cake or a bee. Or directions.

All of the stains you aren't dealing with will be wiped. The lack of stains on your clothes should not be touched.

If they ever do anything they shouldn't, mothers look like bees that you're not happy to see.
Everything they should do is a problem you can't see.

When wiping, the mothers look like children. Like children who know what to do. Like children wiping, or children painting, or children swiping hair from their mothers' faces.

Unless the mothers are upset. Then, while wiping, they look like a pot boiling water.

Just a normal pot of normal boiling water.

If they hide that they are upset, or you are upset with them and not hiding it, or they feel ignored but are not upset about it, or they are thinking about what else they should be wiping, or if they wonder who else could be wiping this, or they are quite happy to be wiping at the moment, or they are pretending to wipe, or they are looking forward to what they will be doing when they are done, or they are talking to themselves, or they are crying, or silent, or saying your name while wiping,

then they look like a pot of boiling water, but with something in it. Like frozen green beans.

Mothers are wiping something without which they would still be mothers. Wiping does not make them mothers, as I just said.

When you see a pot of boiling water, you always see a mother.

WHEN I AM NOT REPEATING MY NAME, I AM REPEATING MY BABY'S NAME. I HAD A BABY.

what is the dailiness in crying especially crying all day what is the dailiness in saying your name and knowing you will have to say it again immediately again because no one ever hears you look what I've done a baby I have to rock I have to tell you what it's like up on my legs babies don't like you to sit but I can't say anything no one wants to hear what is the dailiness no one wants to hear it go on it does not end dailiness ends as in a walk that happens dailiness seems to end as in it happens in a walk on a New York street a smell a fuck a looking good a death a breath or even a trip to the mall or even a memory of one but this keeps going even my trips to the mall I hadn't been in years because we all shop online and because the inside of a mall is like the inside of a bag of shower shoes with eyebrows but it's a place I can bring the stroller is there room for what is wrong as in what people have gotten wrong like a huge pregnant stomach isn't fat I don't mean I'm defending it I mean the body really can move to fit another body inside you don't even have to gain much weight to get that big but you'd prefer to think of it that way instead of thinking of the uterus as something like that is that daily like nothing else it is still with me unlike a baby as in my baby is actually a toddler right now and everyone thinks that's why I'm not writing I'm in the way whatever state I'm in Rhode Island West Virginia Texas Ohio Minnesota I'm in the way but you are in my way and I've never written more since I've had my baby she's already been catcalled this is my baby this is me this is a piece of cake there are 10,000 layers and everyone else this is all three why make it about being a mom like it's both a place no one should want to live in and a place you think everyone privileges that's a lot of mom to fit in the room every day you would know and if I don't ever say who you are we will never know the answer all my writing teachers urged us to say who you are or we will all just be lost because of you and not knowing you

YELLING AT SELFIES

Sometimes we look at art. Sometimes art isn't something you look at. Where is everyone? Everyone is inside Yayoi Kusama's infinity room.

Everyone pretends they are doing this alone. The room is very small, and we can pretend it isn't. The exhibition notes outside said something about love. Something no one would disagree with.

Last week my daughter was corralled into a small space for a lockdown at preschool. Teachers told the children there was a wild animal outside. They waited in the observation booth that's normally used to observe them play. The suspect turned out to be a local who called the police to say, *It's just me chopping wood.*

Once you think too much about what a relief is, you are no longer relieved. Who can I publicly declare this to and then turn away from? Everyone. Three friends are listening. Every day is a public day.

What is experience that stays with you, but not as memory? This is the space of that.

I feel sure. I can feel my posture and am struck that someone wanted to make this space in which I notice my posture. This space wants me to stop and to keep going. We are allowed two minutes.

Susan Sontag says, *Unsure of other responses, they take a picture.*

I take a picture. I post my selfie and think about the likes. It is not a closeup, which is hard to imagine ever posting again. Selfies seem silly after having a child. Please don't think I mean that I neglect myself. As a mother, I have never been more self-absorbed. What else is there to not look at?

I feel hostile towards others lately. I don't want to think too much about it, but I suspect lately means several years. How can I write? Everyone is an audience we post for and don't want near us. What is it to make anything outside of this space?

Who wants to disagree with love? We ask. And then start arguing.

We can crop each other out of our selfies or at least make each other seem really far away. Kusama's mirrors cover us all with polka dots, which the description outside said was unifying. But that is not why we came here.

I'm just like a lot of people, aware of Kusama too many decades into her career. I read a short piece on Kusama's work on the Tate's website that uses the phrase "her feisty attitude." I look at Twitter and read poets' complaints about babies on planes.

I keep opening this poem and looking at it each day until there is no difference between what was happening outside of it when I started writing this poem and what is happening now that I can't finish it. Except four dozen eggs are now in my fridge.

Here I am, outside of the short time I was given inside.

What is the opposite of cracking an egg? This is the space of that.

I WOULD GIVE YOU A DRAWN LINE

There is a line that runs from me to you.

Someone could walk it like a tightrope.

There are a lot of people involved—

Me. You. Whoever came to watch below.

Maybe that French walker, Philippe Petit, who seems like a real jerk.

No one cares, unless they were close to him.

I could be a jerk. I just don't want you over here

because I only understand this line. I know very little

about what keeps us apart. I have seen all of your burger still lifes online.

I don't use a close-up mirror to line my eyes.

Who do I want near me?

I am thinking really hard about one foot in front of the other,

while Philippe's feet just move. Because we are expected to keep

our status updates very brief, I have some time in the week. I walk to work.

I know there's not a first step. I went into an art museum

and stood and looked and decided not to feel stupid about looking.

I decided I like lines more than the figures. Figures make it across, though.

No one looked at me. Many people in the museum seemed proud not to look at the labels.

Shouldn't need them! Don't need them!

I do. What is the title of this line next to another line?

What materials are used to make distance?

What else could you live without? Me?

Dear Reader, I don't want to share you with anyone.

AT NO TIME IN YOUR LIFE, CAN YOU JUST BE NEAR SOMETHING

The world is a mist. And then the world is minute and vast and clear.
—Elizabeth Bishop, "Sandpiper"

Someone will be arguing near you. About what a ghost really is or is not. They will want you to join them and argue. I don't like exchanging ideas through argument or argument disguised as chitchat or high school debate or whatever someone would call it. I don't really like ghosts. I am okay with them, like the color gray in nature. I can feel a whole room this person is in, arguing about ghosts. And I don't want to go in there. There is the sound of someone gluing broken porcelain back together. There are no smells.

In another room is someone who isn't arguing and wouldn't frame considering ghosts as "liking" ghosts. Ghosts are part of the world. They do not care if I go in there or not. I can see this room is full of handouts. Like flyers or homework. The handouts are flying out of the room and over my head. Someone comes by and asks if I have read the handout. I didn't get one, I say. You did not "get" one? They are making fun of my grammar in the doorway of this room that doesn't even belong to them. The person whose room this is is inside teaching a class on printmaking. I often don't think of the uniqueness to an individual print in printmaking. The noun *print* just makes me think *unoriginal*. I want to be writing about things, but I am writing about presence.

Some people around me are not like whole rooms, but like whole worlds. Worlds are less room-like than rooms. A world starts with its breathability and distance. In some ways, there is less to consider, at least immediately. Could I survive here, yes or no. Or maybe before I can even wonder this, water laps my feet.

I am near something, and what do I notice? Every now and then the clouds move past the sun. We say the sun has broken through. I hear someone cough and it sounds like a timid cough. Another's cough asks me how I know. Another is speaking to someone else. One cough reminds me that none of these coughs are speaking to me. Behind me, a cough writes poems just whenever and suddenly has a whole book to publish.

I get further away from what I am near and go online. Online seems like a room or stage, but it is a waterbed. A designer I follow on Instagram whom I'd assume doesn't like Kim Kardashian posts a video of Kim Kardashian. *Look at her eye contact*, she marvels. I let the video play on repeat, trying to see what the designer sees. I see it. Others are moving, but I keep looking, while this bed rolls small waves under me.

Someone is standing next to me in Chicago, taking another picture of The Bean. I take one too, arguing with myself. It is a clear day, so the clouds can't end this poem.

A lot of people aren't talking while together in public. People who aren't talking because they are arguing are rare yet not as interesting as the many people who are together and silent and not arguing. I make a list of all the ways people are together, not talking and not arguing. I start with the people who drift away from each other and still walk around in the same way. Not at the same pace, but as if they are both inside a moment the lights went out. They know what's still there, and they don't.

What am I near? I read Sherod Santos's *Square Inch Hours* over and over again during the pandemic. Writing about changing his daily routine, the speaker says, "Sooner or later the desired sensation of taking my life in my own hands comes over me, and I resume my habits as before." I didn't notice that line until my third reading. It is silly to be so concerned with what you miss until you miss the whole point. But that was not it for me.

I HAVE A MINUTE. COULD YOU HOLD IT?

I guess we don't need another woman explaining why women loathe
catcalling. Everybody knows why. Everybody should know
a number of things, but here is a hand, red from poison oak.
It's reaching out to help me off the bus.
Everyone knows what age we'll sag. When that sound is fireworks or bullets.
Most people will listen when you say it like you are saying it.
You finish the antibiotics, or the infection will come back.
The hunch about Gary from the philosophy department,
I have it, you have it.
The simile for mushrooms invading my houseplants.
Why even go into my classroom and teach.
If I have a baby, it will slide out and say *I know. I already know.*
I probably had a baby. I wasn't invited.
She's already in Dayton, OH, shooting the documentary films that I wanted
     to make.
I wanted to film someone home-birthing or tagging trains. And if I can't,
because I'm thirty-five and wanted to wait just a little longer so I can finish a
     thought
and also this trip to the elliptical machine,
if I can't procreate you can read about it in my next book and be bored.
But everyone knows why we read poetry.
I thought I was done with it,
but I'm still writing about what is between us.
These overlooked states that are most of a country.
When you hold a newborn, and I've got what you've already figured out.
All of this Purell. This old whistle *baby baby*. This new way to call you my
     BFF.
Lana, can you not see the look on my face? Sometimes you are Lana,
talking at me for three hours about how you banged the real-life
Kramer. You've charged me your drinks.
Lana, believe that I'm actually a terrible listener, that we have bad chemistry!
I hate right moves. Like chin up, tits out. Nods over noise. Confidence over

that line you wrote. Everyone loves it. Everybody knows you should.
Don't remind someone they've already told this story.
My poetic poetry's ringtone is *already already already.*
Just what the world needs, another cynic. Everyone knows what a cynic is.

YELLING AT SNOW

I am the new snowplow of the neighborhood.
I'm yelling to melt it.
I can do it all without syllables.

WHY DESCRIBE A MOMENT WHEN

It is the moment of summer. It is not. The peaches are yelling. It sounds
    like bright water.
        My daughter runs through it in the backyard.
                The season to depart as if we are staying right here.
Don't talk about death! she yells at the breakfast table.
        We pretend we can't find her. We pretend we are going to get her.
           We pretend to be dead and flutter.
She discovers how to open all the windows in the house.
        She cries in the car seat, asking if she will die one day, too.

My daughter has a cut. It's pretend. Like everything, it is real.
        We buy Band-Aids like snacks.
                I buy time and unpackage it and see I need to return
                    it.
I keep setting the table with watercolors.
        I say I like her painting, and I am not looking at it.
           And I mean it.

I am painting myself in. I am so not pretend, I can feel how she feels this
    hug.
        I am adding water to everything.
              She keeps adding water to the color.
She says she is making her own color. It is the color of movement.
        It has filled the room.

                She says, You be a dragon. You be water. I will
                  swim in you. Be dead.
When I know I will never be that good. I haven't bought the perfect
    organizing bins.
        What should I make a to-do?
              One slice and the cheap pool bursts open.
I put air on my list. I receive no pressure from anything.

The look of water. The peaches are yelling. Summer saying
        something to itself.
                        The air on my list. I could list more because this is
                        not a room.

This moves like how brightness moves.
        Like the massive waterfall we think of as static.
                        And my daughter is screaming she can't stand silence.
The moment between hearing a fall in another room
        and hearing the cry
                        is a bright, silent space. You wait and squint and go
                        all at once.
We take a picture in the ER when we know she is okay.

Susan Sontag says a photo is a souvenir and souvenirs refuse experience.
        She was just talking about tourists. She was kind of being a snob.
                She take our dead phones home. We save her tiny ER bracelet,
                        but that is enough.
She saves garbage and hides it around the house.
        The idea of garbage comes from me saying, *That's garbage.*

When she was two, everything was something to throw away.
        Now she asks where her peanut shells are. Yogurt cups, sticker
                scraps, twist ties for bread.
                        I am always washing things that are not souvenirs.
She saves the pits to grow a tree.
        She wants to hear the story about the first time she ate a peach.
                        The peaches were yelling, we tell her, again.

I'm a tree, blow me over! My daughter poses and screams.
        I told my writing teacher once that I don't like memory.
                        She snorted. What, like having one?
My daughter walks slowly through gift shops, tapping each souvenir in the
        shop.

The clerk glaring and bracing and deciding when to step in
and scold me, deciding what is enough.
This poem is a leak, a wind, a fruit stand.
My daughter says when the Band-Aid falls off by itself
she will be better, and she is.

HARD CONTAINERS

You need a container. You need something to hold this. A container doesn't have an appetite. I have an appetite I didn't consider ways I'd contain.

You don't need anything for an appetite. It's a requirement that you need nothing in your body.

Even when it's empty, the container holds the idea of containment. Like a confident formula for an unwritten mystery novel that I still couldn't figure out how to fill.

If I am hungry to give you something, and I am looking for a way to give it to you, what is it I am holding in me?

A body is not a container. Like if I think of my body when I was pregnant.

I have years to figure it out.

Once a doctor told me I was pregnant but empty. There was nothing in the sac. I don't think that was the best way to put it.

I have years. What's the best container for presence?

Like how to swaddle a stranger. Like the new baby, the one who made it, is here. Screaming. They said I'd want to eat her up.

I have everything in containers. In the metal baskets, the folded washcloths I spent weeks picking out. Baby washcloths. The baby creams and ointments in the cubby I designated as the ointment and creams cubby. They were carefully reviewed. Any item I could possibly select had reviews that said *I put the cream on the baby, and the baby just started screaming.*

We thought we'd keep the baby in the crib, but we didn't want to put her down. We couldn't put her down. We held her in shifts. *That's probably not sustainable*, the doctor said calmly. I thought maybe it could be. Maybe this was it for us. Maybe this was what hard was, always being there. Was this the hard part? What was this?

It feels nice to walk into something and know what it is. Like the placard outside an art exhibit, giving us the right direction.

I have walked toward a James Turrell light. I have walked towards a James Turrell light thinking it was more than light! He does different things.

People come in and leave once they know what it is.

People are really dumb about babies. When we're on an airplane and my daughter doesn't cry, people smile and approve of this good baby. *She was so good!* They say at the end. Like I am a lion tamer or muffin baker.

I really have no time. I imagined I'd write a book about before, during, and after having a baby, while it was all happening. I would say it's not okay to take your time. In the first version of this poem, everything was perfect boxes, filled, stacked.

With what? I have time to think about it, I guess. My daughter can now spell her name. Inside this sentence she is already starting to read. She is writing stories without me.

I am filling my pockets with my daughter's garbage. I am taking bites of her food without asking. I am happy but empty. I am kidding. I am folding. I don't want to organize anything I won't open again.

I am just holding this ladder so no one will fall.

IF I COULD GIVE YOU A LINE

You have beaten me to it, giving everyone we know compliments.

Mine come out as Enough with the confidence!
Once someone said Don't worry, you look fertile.
Not that I was fishing,

but I would love to be holding something.
Not a pole, but maybe a building.
A very small building I could never enter.

Have you ever been locked out of
your own hands?

You can see the mess you've made,
but you feel like it's something you're still going to make.

A hand reaches out, and I just try to rhyme.

I have thrown confetti at parties and felt like a cornfield.

You can see the drawing, but you can't enter the lines. But there is the
hand. There is the hand. The hand, the line.

Some things become believable when you can't reach them.

Your body is a chandelier when it can point.

I would like for you to look where I say look.

Rows and rows and rows of impenetrable things, maybe a field of them,
make me happy too.

But I'm a poet, and I can't make anything.

UNLINED PORTRAITS

I thought outlines made us see faces in everything. But it is the interior we spot. Knotted noses on trees, nubby eyes. One mushroom ear blossoming out, not listening to us.

*

Why would I buy expensive curtains that allow light through?

*

I was waiting and waiting and waiting, then I stepped out of the line and went home. I wasn't looking at the others in line, but they all thought *Boy is she mad,* and I wasn't.

*

Tony kept explaining he wrote a portrait with words. That was the point of the poem. What could he explain to us? There was nothing else. We kept looking at it.

*

Wow, you said. Wow. We sure do the same thing differently.

*

That moment when something becomes a line because of what has landed on it. But never from what has left it?

*

Seth says, while he house-sat, he read our writing teacher's daily notebooks. Years stacked out in the open, and they were so boring.

*

When my dentist sighs out of stress, I realize I would rather she sigh from boredom.

*

I kept talking about all of the images in the text, but it was written entirely of things they had said.

*

In Texas, without winter weather, I would completely lose where I was in the year.

*

Winter comes, covers the lines, and makes a field.

*

Describing a moment that sticks with me usually means I have not described anything at all, but when I am done, I feel like I could.

*

Undefined spaces, the joy and lie.

*

Since there is only one direction to read a story, surely we would get to the climax and know it's the climax because it is so obvious.

*

Outside of this line there is the face in the car that was happy to hit me if I took another step in the crosswalk.

*

Every email ending with *Please advise.*

*

No one really walks through fields. They just stand outside of them and look.

INSIDE A MAP OF ARNOLD SCHWARZENEGGER'S ARM

I map my arm as if it can be a map, too.
I want to see my arm inside of his,
to arm wrestle for territory with his best arm, his younger one,
his arm that can't move while I map mine inside.

I will never contain the secret to mind-blowing arms
within this map of my arm inside his, but every map has resources.
To know my house, I make a map of all of its blue.
To understand my potential,
I make a map of tomorrow and navigate it when the real day happens,
but my map and the real day never match.

How to approach tomorrow takes a long time.
About the same time it takes to find everything blue in my house,
which is not as long as it takes to build up great arms.
For something that requires a lot of time, pumping iron really lacks mystery.
You either work on your arms, or you don't—you know how it goes.

I love the map of my arm inside Arnold's, because there is nowhere to go.
Like being in a room built entirely for blue things. Like building a house, a
tiny house just around the top of my house, around the weather vane, where
you go up and visit and just look at it, without the weather to direct it.

IF THIS WERE A SCULPTURE, I COULD WALK AROUND TO SEE ALL OF ITS SIDES

I think about holding the door for you at the same time I have already gone inside. In fact, I am holding the door right now, because I feel bad about it. Even though it is not the same. It is not the same as waiting too long to hold the door in the first place. The first place I waited was inside of myself.

There isn't a second place,

but everything moves along like there will be.

It's a story feeling.

The story doesn't wait. It promises to take you. You wait and listen.
You are allowed to go. To think about others. To not think about others.

Where would we be without you.

In class, we read Sei Shōnagon, and I assign students their own lists of Hateful Things—
I hate it when drivers let too many cars merge. And I hate it when I'm holding a door and you don't even say Thank you my god how hard is it.

When any storm rolls in, it shows up like it has years of experience.

What will we do differently next time. The tree broke a limb during the last storm, and we pay too much money to have it trimmed when we know the whole thing needs to go down.

The winds in Rhode Island are always gale winds. In Minnesota they are just gusty. They are the winds I base all winds on. In Washington, they are fire hazards. When I lived there, I didn't live on the rainy side of Washington state, and so many people look puzzled when I say this. A few insist I'm mistaken.

Then, nothing happens. It rushes everyone. It's a still moment. The whole place must be raining.

Someone suggested news stories as a way of writing about something else because all of this will eventually end. After she said this, we ordered lunch, and I mispronounced *niçoise*. This was in Ohio, twenty years ago.

We have empathy for people who have held things in for too long. When close, we have little patience for people who won't let things go. When my daughter was a baby, someone asked if she was a good person. Like a good baby? Fussy? *No. Like how some people are bad, you know.*

I know how the right space between you and me, when I've let go at the right moment, turning away, will land the door somewhat gently in your hands.

My teacher said, look, you've arranged things in such a way that to address any problem in here would destroy everything.

I throw so many precious things away when my daughter isn't looking. There isn't enough room to hang on to it. There's enough time, just not enough room.

HARD AND SOFT MATERIALS USED TO MAKE DISTANCE

Push to decline. A beg. A plan. A breast feeding.

The weeds. A child will not keep their distance. They will run into the
weeds.

Someone yelling get out of the weeds. Someone feels hard and soft and not
close.

A jacket. A sneeze. A stomp.

Those kinds of sighs that repel. The perfumes we can afford. A window.

The softness of a twirl doesn't seem distant, but we can't get close.

It is in my arms, just crying at me.

A big stone thing as soon as you walk in the museum.

I have no response but joy.

Inside an egg. Outside of a line.

The clouds are breaking apart.

A baby's crawl. I have argued with bees.

All the lines like I don't know, where do you want to eat?

A mutter in the bouquet. *Speak up,* they say, swimming away.

A flock of butterflies for a list.

THE ROPED YEARS

After the age of disconnection came the age of connection.

One couple tied each end of a three-foot rope around a wrist. They connected.

They touched each other less. They touched each other more. They pretended not to know each other. They decided not to know each other. They decided not to touch. They touched. They found their rules. They broke them. They danced.

They worked from home, which was convenient, that this worked out. They weren't trying to destroy their lives or anything.

Some evenings he sketched her. She drew over it.
They made sentences as long as the rope.

This wasn't competitive or a sedative, an adjective or a noun.
This wasn't, *How do you go to the bathroom?* Wasn't kink. Wasn't exhibition.

Could this be about anything else than intimacy?

Whether the other ate or not, they never dined alone.

They didn't talk one day, all day, then a few days, seeing if they could read each other's minds. I am trying to read you. I am trying to read you! It became a line for a while,

but the rope, always one.
A line of what to do, not what to say.

The rope not as telephone string or psychic cord.
Not a symbol of intimacy.
Not a connection through confessions, obsessions, secrets, mindreading.

They used the rope to lasso each other.
They stood apart and made fractions.
The rope as border, this side and that side, on the bed,
across the shower, on the supermarket floor.

Other people said the couple was stupid, which brought these other people
closer together.

WOULD YOU HOLD THIS EGG, PLEASE?

This is an encyclopedia of holding.

This is a fashion spread of eggs that were held and eggs that were not held.

This is a time machine to go back to every moment you were asked a favor
and wonder if it was actually a favor.

Will you tell me if there's anything I can do?
Will you tell me if I offend you?
                It's as easy as machine gun practice on eggs for targets.
Let me know if my cat's scratch leaves a scar.

Those friends aren't doing you a favor,

nor those stripes on that shirt, nor chuckling to yourself
about looking ugly wearing stripes, nor rolling your eyes
at anyone who attempts to make you chuckle.
Your eyes are a letdown, too,
because they're a better blue than your shirt's stripes.

Those lips aren't doing you a favor,
but they sure make you look good. I bet you know what it looks like
when they speak to others and you talk to yourself, that you simply talk
to yourself because it feels beautiful to know you look good.

Someone told me the definition of narcissism
is to know what you look like when you're talking to someone else.

A moment on the lips, a lifetime on the hips, he said one other time.
Some people would consider this warning a compliment,
but only if you are too beautiful to wreck yourself with a second dessert.

The moment I eat all the desserts
I'll become all the hips, an encyclopedia of lifetimes.
Look at all these references to the times we've been held.

DON'T WAKE UP THE PAINTINGS

Sometimes I want to be everything but impressive. My walk is artless. A common duck, always unfilmed. I am always waiting to be. I am always.

Impressed, I pace the artist in my neighborhood who walks with a busted can of paint. A line of paint following him, he only looks forward.

I like his emotions. There are none. Perhaps many. Nobody watches what we're doing. Like I have permission to get it wrong.

All I ever used to do was wait to be moved. And be told what to do. Now I fear this is how I'm going to impress you.

I hope the age of Is It Art or Not? is becoming Want to Go for a Walk?

I have feelings. I write them about people. Does that mean I have to live in the suburbs?
I fall in line with an artist, so maybe you think I live somewhere worth something.

I have students without teeth or safety. Our tap water is a gimmick in a postmodern plot. Our mayor promotes deer hunting from sidewalks. There's a bullet hole through the little bell on my cat's collar.

Between thinking and action there should be a bell. But we lost the little ball that makes that bell jangle.

I already broke into sincerity, and no one seemed to care. I was free to touch the art and swim in the pool unattended.

A FEW THINGS I DID WELL, OR AT LEAST BETTER THAN WHAT WAS POSSIBLE

Sawed a hotdog, cradled glue, stopped a hurricane, and started a hunger.
Ironed my dress on Mt. Everest. There's the dirt I made you. The ice I
hugged, the current I kicked, the transition I clung to. Really, there was
no stopping it— I just challenged that hurricane. Stapled five hundred
desk fans to my roof. Threw sawdust. Sneezed. Fell over for total fake out.
I did a great deal of staring at the sun as a child, but I'm not certain it was
a primer in bravery, stupidity, or how to lose. To this day I can squint the
alphabet. Until I realized it was reflex, everyone I loved was the letter E.
Yes, you— bright as Houston sun without all the rain. I'm working on my
own appearance. I pose like a horseshoe, waiting to be flung. How lucky
to be mistaken for a cactus and still hugged. I've studied flinches, dated
double takes, interviewed winks. Failing to craft a handbook on perception,
I composed a score for a chorus of blinks.

THERE ARE PLACES AND ACTIVITIES THAT MAKE SENSE TO RETURN TO, AND I OFTEN RUIN THOSE THE FIRST TIME BY SAYING, *NEXT TIME WE COME WE WILL . . .*

The idea of Rothko's Chapel attracts you. When inside, the paintings seem to say, look you're on your own. You are happy to be on your own. Are you happy to be on your own? Next time we come we will explain ourselves. Next time we come we will not know why we came.

These moments involve other people. I can't stand to hear myself say this to someone else, but I am always saying it to someone who just goes with it. When my husband and I are excited about somewhere we've gone, no one can stand to hear about it.

I imagine people are different there, a mom says at a birthday party. I spend too many minutes explaining how the people in Minnesota farmland are their own rooms, until I start creating one for myself. Later, I consider she might've just been asking how backwards they are. Maybe if they are just nicer. Maybe if she could simply get me to talk. We are in New England, a place where I'm to live in the idea of New England and ignore all its failings.

The first layer underneath anything is the plains. It is under any place I am in because I grew up in the plains. I could stand on the road within the southern Minnesota plains and see anything coming my way for a few miles. I couldn't wait to leave, but that is not how leaving works. What could unexpectedly happen when you could see it approaching for over a mile? Probably something, but I couldn't see that.

As often as I wanted, I could visit Rothko's Chapel when I lived in Houston. I remember the details of it less than how people talked about it before I went and after I went. I picture four large canvases, but there are fourteen. It was his last major work, and he knew what would happen to him when he finished, everyone says. It was airless and doomed and dark purple. Some found it peaceful. Friends have argued with other friends about what to take away from it. It was a place for meditation, reflection, dread, silence, dialogue.

Houston is where I met my husband. Also, where I looked at a lot of art every week. What of your experiences are hard to explain? It was a city of glass and corners and other things you don't hang on to. I wouldn't think being surprised would be hard to explain. A lot of surprises are just what we want to happen, finally happening. That was not what this was.

My husband and I don't need to leave a party anymore to reflect on others. On Twitter, I scroll past a post on liminal spaces. I've seen this account before, but sometimes the photographed spaces aren't liminal. They are just spaces at a moment without people.

Inside Ragnar Kjartansson's art video, *The Visitors,* you can choose where to stand and listen and watch. It shows nine screens at once of the same place, an old Victorian mansion in rural New York. Each musician is in a different room performing and singing the same song together. It is too romantic, almost embarrassing. But the longer I stayed the more space I felt inside of it, while riding through its repetitions. It didn't feel like I could stay too long. Viewers exiting the space didn't seem to argue about what to take away from it, but no one was agreeing.

There are places that don't make sense to return to. I returned to the site of my daughter's preschool graduation the day after. I wasn't hanging on. Everything was right there, really far away. I did feel sad and didn't want to ruin that feeling, but that was not remembering. I was curious about being in the wrong place or, really, one that didn't have anything for me anymore.

WAYS TO KEEP SELF-PORTRAITING

I assembled a me from them. I assembled a you.
We know all the lines. I've drawn the negative space around each one.

I can't draw myself because I can't fit on the paper.

Someone said I look like Kiefer Sutherland and all of the Midwestern
plains. Nobody can decide where the Midwest ends.

But what is the line for *you are not alone,* not at all said like we've said it
    before?

Like when we're just saying anything instead of just saying anything.

I am an artist who has drawn every inch of herself except for what she looks
    like.

One day we will not know Kiefer Sutherland! My portraits will just evoke
    chipmunk cheeks.
You say only chipmunk cheeks will remain. As chipmunk cheeks!

I have made nothing but what's identifiable.

I made a mold of myself and cast several mes. In soap, in disco balls, in a
    chessboard set.
I poured in the entire state of Iowa, which you point out is clearly
    Midwestern.

I meet myself in cheese and just want crackers.

Are you sure you want to eat that?

I have taken that line. I have collected all the tones—

Nice haircut. I mean, nice try.
That's something different. I've seen it before.
You look like I used to, like when I was staying indoors.
It was a tremendous time! Those pants should go nowhere.

How would you make a sculpture out of *Tell me something I don't know?*

The line you say as saying something still unsaid—

What kind of portrait would look like that?

I'd like to make a self-portrait you'd prefer.

A breaking bust,
something you can keep pushing off the pedestal display?

Self-portrait as It once had a striking resemblance! It once had a striking resemblance! It once had a striking resemblance!

DIRECTION

I saw a bell on our walks and then I saw other bells

none of them were ringing

some were for emergencies, and some were for joy

some were to keep us away, and some to bring us in

everything was close

everything else was not leaving

which direction

the distance of union and fire and worship

what was close

the mailman with no mail

parents pretending to get up from chairs

any hand in traffic

a wave that's just wind

retaining walls crumbling as planned

my daughter's slap-footed run

treadmills through the windows and glass in the street

our stone collection in the stroller

more in her hands some down my shirt.

where will they go the stones will have to go

we stack some as tall as our mouths

why wait for a ringing we're not we are running

we can't think of a better way to not be a tree.

CATAPULTING A LIGHT POLE THROUGH THE AIR WOULD BE THE MOST BEAUTIFUL SHOOTING STAR

I used to think all of this was about the impossible. An attraction to chairs made of bubble wrap and denim canoes. Or identical tears. Crying tears upward.

That I can't slingshot a light pole through the air. How I wanted to. SlingSHOOT? Shooting star.

You can indeed, however, sling and fling a light pole through the air. You need the right tools and materials. I don't have the right tools, and I don't want to learn how to build these things.

I thought I did.
Because it's possible, now I don't want to do it?

Action, action, action.

I thought I just couldn't find the patience to build whimsy—that this lack of patience was about failed desires.
        But I didn't give up on anything.

I love the idea of a glass hammer and nails. If you made these, I love that you thought it was impossible, and now here they are. But you were mistaken, because here they are.

This is a poem that wants nothing.

I love the idea of it, and this love is not inaction. It's not action, either. But it's not lacking action.

Unrelated, everything is succeeding.

Unrelated, everyone is convinced they are actions, they are moving, and thus something is right, perfect, just normal enough to look up at night skies.

A PRECISE, NEW BEGINNING

I sew a shirt out of fresh envelopes.

I make a day planner on rows of little baby corn.

When I'm a man, I give childbirth.

I Instagram my first word. I baptize balloons.

What do you call it when you shit the pot you were sitting on?
The moment when you put on pants instead of writing them a letter?

Never has there been such a blurred middle/end/beginning
as when I'm surrounded by threads.

Shuffling, braiding, affording it.

You end up singing like Wanda Jackson instead of Peggy Lee.
Is it whom you listen to or do you just start singing it?

I collect the ways clouds break apart.
I call it the moment you startle the cirrus.

Again and again and again,
I've burned everything I've written. Like a big deal,

like this is such the moment.
To get over. To pull the bus cord. And I can smell myself.

I call this the pre-menopause hairdo for newborn babies.

I write a word with styling gel and just light a match. A lungful.
I call it a lungful.

IMPOSSIBLE HOLDS SUCCESSFULLY HELD

I was busy worrying about the rat. Then, if the sky would stop changing. Then my locked unemployment account. How to say that I am not a young lady.

I was at no time close to letting go, but I was not holding anything. I wasn't the wind, but I felt across landscapes.

I was not waiting. I didn't know how to wait anymore, which is a kind of waiting.

It didn't seem like want. Want is for something far away.

Birds are always in the back yard. We don't need to attract them. My dad sent us a birdfeeder, because where he lives, there are few birds, and they need to be drawn in. One morning I saw squirrels crack open the birdfeeder, and then I saw a rat eating out of it.

I knew that my unopened files would not hold my thoughts, because I had no thoughts.

When I finally had some free time, I painted my office ceiling. My husband came in to see. Before he could say it looked nice, I said I knew it looked the same as before. It had taken six hours.

Every day I feel joy knowing nearly invisible blemishes have been painted over.

My daughter says she can't stand her white bedroom walls. They are swallowing her eyes.

I look her in the eyes throughout the day, to connect. I have a hard time completely losing myself in parenthood. Unless parenthood is continuously thinking, I am a parent. Also, I apologize a lot.

I point out the color in her room. But this is not about looking at it. She says she wants to buy me a yellow bear so I can remember my childhood. She says she is working on her fears. Then says she's over her fears and will never be afraid again.

There can't be two skies in one painting, but that's what these moments feel like. Then she points out a bug and is scared. There isn't a bug, I say, then see it. She is always right.

There is something buoying. Everything sinks except this feeling of what buoys around me. It's not always the same thing buoying. I can't even understand what it all is. I am not holding on to any of it, but I am not sinking. This is how it is all the time.

This is not the opposite of one time. One time in a Quaker meeting house, my husband and I looked up at dusk, the ceiling cut out in a perfect frame by James Turrell. Our eyes held by the changing sky, but we did not lose them.

We weren't watching, really. When watching, you wait to see if you are right or wrong. Here, nothing was hiding, but I kept forgetting that. It kept me from making lists of what I thought was happening.

I MADE A DINNER PARTY CENTERPIECE ENTIRELY OUT OF YOU. ARE YOU COMING?

Would you come to my party at the very end of the party?
I haven't even said anything, but come closer.
I haven't even said anything, but could you make something with this.
I've already made you without anything. Hello, but even better.
Basically: here I am, here I am.
Here is now, and here is an actual now.
Here is a desire, and here is an actual desire. Is it yours or mine. My fingers
    are gone.

We're never going to meet, so why not set my poem on fire.
I have to be in stories, but not in here.
Here is yearning, and here is actual yearning.
This line is playing a song. Finally, we can just feel things.
This line is hungry, but this line just waited too long to eat.
I've eaten it, along with my fingers.

When I'm at the edge of the pool, I'm in the pool, but not the other way
    around.

Push me in. I want you here and there. I want you authentic and fake.
I want you mechanically and hand-drawn.
You've pulled me in closer, by just chopping wood. The exact technique and
surprise breaks. We can see it. There's a pile of wood. It's an Agnes Martin.
It's on fire and pastel.
I got this feeling while frightened. I was near others. But it was a quiet
    museum.

Should I run or become a grid.

You do this by drawing your lines.
I follow without a body.
You've pulled me in closer, just by wavering. I thought I wanted an RSVP.

Works Referenced

"A Bunch of Different Parts Can Make Up Ekphrasis, Including a Scoff When I Round the Museum Corner with My Baby in the Stroller. Or the Invisible Push to Keep Moving that Means Keep Looking, Like Stop Looking. Or the Things I Think of When I Look at Art and Won't Ever Explain, Even" quotes two lines (in italics) from Sylvia Plath's "Morning Song."

"Yelling at Selfies" quotes a line (in italics) from "On Photography," by Susan Sontag." It also quotes from "Who is Yayoi Kusama?" https://www.tate.org.uk/kids/explore/who-is/who-yayoi-kusama.

"Why Describe a Moment When" references lines from "On Photography," by Susan Sontag.

"The Roped Years" was influenced by Linda Montano and Tehching Hsieh's year-long performance, *Rope Piece*.

"Catapulting a Light Pole Through the Air Would be the Most Beautiful Shooting Star" was influenced by Michael Sailstorfer's documented artwork, *Shooting Star*.

Acknowledgements

The following poems have appeared in these publications:

The Awl: "Ways to Keep Self-Portraiting"

Bennington Review: "I Kept a Voice in My Peacock" and "A Bunch of Different Parts Can Make up Ekphrasis, Including Your Scoff When I Round the Museum Corner With My Baby In The Stroller. Or The Invisible Push To Keep Moving That Means Keep Looking, Like Stop Looking. Or The Things I Think of When I Look At Art and Won't Ever Explain, Even."

Boog City: "Yelling at Selfies," "Why Describe a Moment When," and "Unlined Portraits"

cellpoems: "Yelling at Snow"

Columbia Poetry Review: "I Have a Minute. Could You Hold it?"

Connotation Press: An Online Artifact: "The Roped Years" and "Catapulting a Light Pole Through the Air Would Make the Most Beautiful Shooting Star"

Denver Quarterly: "Inside a Map of Arnold Schwarzenegger's Arm"

DIAGRAM: "Any Time You Want, You Can See Mothers Wiping"

the fanzine: "Would You Hold this Egg, Please?"

The Laurel Review: "A Few Things I Did Well, Or At Least Better Than What Was Possible," "I Made a Dinner Part Centerpiece Entirely Out of You. Are You Coming?" and "If This Were a Sculpture, I Could Walk Around to See All of Its Sides."

Miracle Monocle: "If I Could Give You a Line" and "I Would Give You a Drawn Line"

Pangyrus: "Will You Line up the Children?"

Pleiades: "A Precise, New Beginning"

Privacy Policy: An Anthology of Surveillance Poetics: "Don't Wake Up the Paintings"

Sixth Finch: "Impossible Holds Successfully Held"

Thank you to the Rhode Island State Council on the Arts for their support through the award of their 2020 Fellowship in Poetry. I could not have completed this book without your support.

Thank you to Mary Biddinger, Erika Meitner, Mary-Kim Arnold, and Graham Foust.

Love and thanks to Kent Shaw, my first and best reader.

Photo: Charlie Peters

Carrie Oeding is the author of *Our List of Solutions* (42 Miles Press), which won the Lester M. Wolfson Prize. She was the recipient of the 2020 Rhode Island State Council on the Arts' Fellowship in Poetry. Her work has appeared in such places as *Bennington Review, Denver Quarterly, Colorado Review, Pleiades, Mid-American Review,* and *DIAGRAM.* She grew up on a southern Minnesota farm and lives in Rhode Island.